Alas, Dear Reader

A Play

Valerie Maskell

A SAMUEL FRENCH ACTING EDITION

SAMUEL FRENCH

FOUNDED 1830

SAMUELFRENCH-LONDON.CO.UK
SAMUELFRENCH.COM

CHARACTERS

Agnes Bristow
Lucy Smith, her spinster sister
Dora Bristow, Agnes's eighteen-year-old daughter
Hattie Bristow, her twelve-year-old sister
Jessie Plumb, Hattie's governess

The action takes place in the parlour of the Bristow's house

Period—Victorian

ALAS, DEAR READER

The scene is a small, crowded mid-Victorian parlour, complete with both lace and velvet curtains, an aspidistra in a pot, a draped mantelshelf, overmantel and so on. There is a bright fire in the fireplace down R, an oil lamp on the table, as well as gas lamps over the mantelpiece and the light is reasonably bright and the atmosphere cosy. The window is centre back and the door to the hall down L

When the Curtain *rises Agnes is reclining on the chaise-longue and Lucy sits in an armchair. Hattie, clasping her doll, sits on a footstool near the fire and Dora and Jessie are seated at the table. Dora is sewing rather clumsily and Jessie is reading aloud*

Jessie ". . . and Sir Edward stood before me, tall and handsome, with the kindest eyes in the whole world. As he took my hand in his I knew that Lady Christabel's Crime was forgotten and with God's help and grace I would prove a fitting helpmeet for the heir to Wentworth Park."

Lucy Ah, how lovely. (*Wiping her eyes*) I do like a happy ending.

Hattie Well, I wouldn't have married him, not after the way he let her down.

Dora Of course you would, silly. Think of his money.

Agnes Really, Dora, how can you say such a thing. Christabel married William because she loved him.

Dora Love him or not, I don't suppose she had to mend any more stockings.

Agnes Anyway, it was a lovely story, and you read beautifully, Jessie.

Lucy Such expression.

Hattie It isn't time to stop yet. Have we got another book?

Dora There are two under mamma's cushion. One by the same author, Mrs Arthur Beech.

Hattie rises eagerly and finds two library books, hidden behind a cushion on the chaise-longue

Hattie This looks good. "Lady Dorothy's Dilemma, Vol. 1."

Lucy "Lady Dorothy's Dilemma"? Oh, I think we've had that before.

Hattie (*looking into the book*) Oh, yes, we have. It's about a wicked governess who poisons a countess. Oh Dora, you are stupid. Fancy getting one we've already read.

Agnes Hattie, that's enough. Dora can't possibly remember all the books we've had out. What's the other one?

Dora We haven't had *that* one, I'm sure. Hattie's thinking about "The Tangled Web". That was the one about the governess. And it wasn't by Mrs Beech. It was by E.L.

Hattie E.L. who?

Dora Just E.L., silly.

Agnes Dora, you're as bad as Hattie.

Jessie (*soothingly*) We've read so many now. They're all getting mixed up.

Hattie I'm not mixing them up. I can remember them all. There was "Lady Mary's Mistake" about the long-lost twin brother coming home and saving her from worse than death . . .

Agnes Hattie . . .

Hattie And "The Lytch Gate". That was where Lady Caroline ran off with the under-gardener, and they lived in an attic and he died and her mother went into a decline . . .

Lucy I didn't like that, it was too miserable.

Hattie Well, life is mostly miserable.

Agnes Hattie, what a wicked thing to say.

Hattie I don't see why. We're not very happy, are we? With father in the way of every single thing we want to do. We can't have a kitten. Or go and listen to the band. Or have anyone to tea. And Dora's not allowed even to see Teddy, let alone marry him, and if she ran off with him it would be just like Lady Caroline and . . .

Dora Of course it wouldn't. I'm not a duke's daughter and Teddy's a bank clerk not an under-gardener . . .

Hattie No, but father's just as horrible as the duke. Horribler.

Agnes Hattie, don't say such things. There's no such word as "horribler". It should be "more horrible".

Hattie "More horrible", then. Anyway, are we going to start a new one or not? He'll be home soon.

Lucy Oh, do let's. We've nearly half an hour.

Dora Come on then or we shall have nothing to think about. Let's try this one.
Hattie What's it called?
Jessie "The Purple Flower" by E.L.
Hattie I don't like the sound of it. I like them best when they're called Lady somebody's something.
Agnes Be quiet, darling.
Jessie (*reading*) "The Purple Flower. Chapter one. A chill mist lay over the ancestral home of the Mannerings. In the tower bedroom Lady Anne . . ."
Hattie Oh good.
Dora }
Lucy } SSSH! { *Together*
Jessie "...Lady Anne lay asleep."

A noise is heard from the street

(*Looking up*) What was that?
Dora Nothing. Go on.
Agnes Better just peep through the curtains, Hattie . . .

Hattie rises, leaving her doll by the fire, and moves to the window

Hattie Not a soul's in sight, except a cab stopped on the other side of the road. Oh, and the muffin man. Oh, Mother, couldn't we have some muffins? Just for once?
Agnes No dear, what on earth would father say? Come and sit by me. You're scorching your face.

Hattie perches by her mother

Hattie Oh, bother father. We never have anything nice. Come on, Miss Plumb, we must get into the story before he comes.
Jessie Do you think I ought to stop, Mrs Bristow?
Agnes We'll be all right for ten minutes.
Jessie Very well. "In the blue-draped cradle at the foot of the bed lay a tiny creature no bigger than a bird."
Hattie What kind of bird?
Lucy Hattie . . .
Dora Oh what does it matter what kind of bird?
Hattie Well, it makes a difference, doesn't it? It might be a sparrow or an ostrich.

Agnes Try not to be silly, dear. It means a medium-sized bird. Like a crow.

Hattie Then why doesn't it say a little creature no bigger than a crow?

Dora Oh, for goodness' sake . . .

Hattie Well, when I do my composition Miss Plumb always says I must put exactly what I mean, don't you, Miss Plumb?

Jessie Well yes I do, Hattie, but if you're not quiet I can't go on with the story.

Hattie All right, but still.

Jessie "With tears in his eyes Lord Wallingford gazed at his new-born child. A girl. His dissolute younger brother Percy was still the heir. Lady Anne's eyelids fluttered . . ."

The front door is heard to open and close. Heavy footsteps pass the door and they all sit frozen with horror. There is a pause

Hattie (*whispering*) He's hanging up his coat.

Dora He's jolly early.

Lucy Thank goodness I left the kettle on the back of the range.

Dora That must have been him in the cab.

The footsteps continue up the hall and then a door is heard to open and close

Lucy He's gone into the study. I'd better go and see to his tea.

Agnes Put the books away quickly. Jessie, you and Hattie go up to the schoolroom. Dora, pass me that book of sermons and turn the lamp down.

Lucy goes out

Hattie hides the books behind the cushion and Jessie hurries her out of the room

Dora gives Agnes the book of sermons from the table, turns the lamp down and then sits

(*Opening the book at random and reading*) ". . . and I say unto you, blessed are ye that have wholesome bread, for ye have no need of dainties, honoured are ye who wear homespun, for ye are warmer than they who wear silk and lace, beloved are ye who wash in cold water, for ye are purer than they . . ."

Dora It's all right, Mamma, he won't come in now.

Agnes You never know, if he has to wait for his tea . . .

Dora I wonder why he came home so early?

Agnes I don't remember the last time he took a cab. I wonder if he's ill.

Dora Mamma, if he's in a good mood tonight, will you try again?

Agnes Try again?

Dora About Teddy, I mean. Ask if Teddy can come and see him. Tell him he's been promoted.

Agnes Oh, dear, I really don't think it will be any good.

Dora But why not? Why not?

Agnes I don't know, except that it's not his idea. Teddy seems a nice boy to me. Dora, do go and help Aunt Lucy, she gets so flustered. Pass me your sewing. I'll do a little for you.

Dora (*taking the sewing to Agnes*) Mamma, do listen. I'm nearly nineteen—and I've got to get married sometime, haven't it? Or I'll end up like Aunt Lucy!

Agnes Dora, what have you done to this? I think you've joined the sleeve to the neckband. Oh dear, you never think what you're doing.

Dora Mamma, *please*, I'm going round to the Bainbridges' before supper.

Agnes You mustn't go out tonight, it's far too late.

Dora Jessie can come with me. After all, Gertie Bainbridge is my oldest friend—well, my only friend, I suppose.

Agnes Darling, if father found out that Jessie had gone to the Bainbridges' with you, he'd probably dismiss her; and she wouldn't find it easy to get another post. She's a sweet girl but not really a very good governess.

Dora But he needn't find out, need he, Mamma, if you tell him we've gone to choir practice? That's about the only thing we are allowed to do.

Agnes I cannot tell lies for you, Dora, you know that would be very wrong.

Dora (*wheedling*) But you won't be telling lies, darling Mamma. We always sing round the piano at the Bainbridges'. You should hear Teddy.

Agnes It's not choir practice.

Dora Well, it's singing. Why should "Come into the Garden Maud" be any more wicked than "All Things Bright and Beautiful"? Father's just got this idea that anything nice is wrong. Just because he wasn't allowed to have any fun when he was young.

Lucy comes in

Lucy (*very agitated*) Agnes. The key of the store cupboard—
   quick. I must get out some Gentleman's Relish. I only hope he
   doesn't notice it's a new pot. He said last night there was enough
   left for today. I suppose Hattie's been at it again.
Dora Well, why shouldn't she? Why shouldn't we all have it if
   we like it?
Agnes It's far too expensive for us all.
Dora Then let him have plum jam like us.
Agnes (*detaching a key from a bunch, which she has taken out of
   her pocket*) He is the breadwinner, dear.
Dora And the Gentleman's Relish winner too.
Lucy (*taking the key*) Oh Lord, what will he say? And his tea
   not ready. How was I to know he was coming home early.

Lucy goes out

Agnes I do wish he wouldn't treat her as a servant. She is my
   sister.
Dora He doesn't even do that. Servants get paid.

Hattie comes in

Hattie I left Arabella.
Dora (*nastily*) You're too big for dolls.
Hattie Mind your own business. (*She puts her tongue out at Dora*)
Agnes Girls, girls, I do wish . . .

Hattie lets out a wail, as she picks up the doll from near the fire

Hattie Oooh look, she's melted. Oooh Arabella!
Agnes Oh dear. I told you not to leave her in front of the fire.
Hattie Her face has gone all squashy. Oh, dash! Bother! I wish I
   knew some really bad words.
Agnes Hattie, be quiet do. You'll have father in here. Give her
   to me. Perhaps I can do something.
Hattie (*weeping*) It's no good. She's too far gone.
Dora (*looking at the doll*) Unless you want to do some witchcraft.
Hattie Witchcraft!
Dora You know—like in—oh what was it—? Where she made a
   wax model of her father's second wife and stuck pins into its
   heart . . .

Hattie Oh yes, "The Stepmother", I remember.
Agnes What nonsense you're talking, children. Who on earth would Hattie want to make a wax model of?

There is a short pause as the same thought occurs to each of them

Hattie Well, I'm not going to stick pins into bits of Arabella. Anyway, there wouldn't be enough wax, would there?
Dora You could make quite a small model. They don't have to be any special size.
Hattie I expect people use candles. Except that they're so white. I wonder if it makes a difference—the colour?
Dora Sure to. If you wanted to kill a black man you'd have to get black wax, wouldn't you?
Agnes Do stop it, children, please. Sometimes I wonder where you get it all. Now let me look at Arabella. Perhaps we could get her a new head.
Hattie No, I should hate her with a new head. It wouldn't be Arabella.
Agnes You'd soon get used to it.
Hattie I wouldn't. If my head got cut off in an accident and doctors sewed a . . .
Dora Hattie, stop it. Make her be quiet, Mamma, or I shall be sick.
Hattie You're a baby. You wouldn't be any good as a nurse. Nurses have to look at blood, and bits of legs . . .
Dora Stop it. (*She puts her hand over Hattie's mouth*)
They struggle
Agnes Stop it at once. Hattie! Dora! You'll have father in here.
Dora No we shan't. He'll be having his tea, in front of the study fire. Then he'll hear Hattie's lesson. Then he'll go upstairs and change into his smoking-jacket. Then at nine o'clock he'll go to the club. There's one thing about father, we do know what he's going to do.
Hattie That's just the trouble. The same thing every day, never anything different.
Dora If it was different it might be worse. At least we're on our own for quite a lot of the time, and we can read our books.
Agnes That's right, dear, look on the bright side. Now run upstairs, Hattie, and tidy your hair.
Hattie (*taking her doll*) Oh poor Arabella! I've murdered you. I

wish you didn't look so horrible. Can I leave the door open?
It's so dark.

Agnes Yes, only go *on*!

Hattie goes out

Poor child. She really loves that doll. It's her main pleasure in
life. I shall have to get something done about it.

Dora At least she's got some pleasure. Even father can't object
to her playing with dolls.

Agnes Cheer up, darling. Tomorrow we'll be able to go on with
the book. I think this one about Lady Anne sounds really
exciting. You can get your work done early, and we'll have a
good long . . .

Lucy comes in closing the door behind her

Lucy Agnes! Dora! The most terrible news. Oh, what are we
going to do?

Lucy sits down, quite distraught, and Dora goes to her

Agnes Lucy, dear, what is it? What has happened? Have you
broken something?

Lucy Worse than that. Far worse. Oh, dear! (*She starts to cry*)

Agnes What is it then, is something on fire?

Lucy No, no, it's nothing I've done. I wish it were. (*Between
sobs*) He's RETIRED!

Dora You mean—gone to bed?

Lucy No, no no, I mean he's retired from business. For good.

Agnes Retired from business? But how can he? What about the
shop?

Lucy He sold it. Six weeks ago, he says. He handed it over today.

Agnes But, why didn't he tell me?

Lucy It's like him, isn't it? Why should he tell you?

Dora But what will he do all day? Won't he be going to the shop
anymore?

Lucy Of course not. It belongs to somebody else now. He'll be
here, won't he?

Agnes All the time.

Lucy Oh what have I done to deserve this? There won't be a
moment's peace. I think I shall go into a decline.

Agnes That's out of the question, dear. (*Firmly*) You should thank God for your good health. If only I were well and strong . . .

The door opens and Hattie puts her head in

Hattie I'm just going to say my French verbs to father.
Agnes I hope you know them.
Hattie Well I think I do. But I always forget when I'm in there and he walks up and down and says great heavens he's reared a half-wit.
Agnes Never mind, dear, you must be glad he takes such an interest in your education.
Dora He'll probably take even more interest from now on.
Hattie (*coming further into the room*) What d'you mean?
Dora When he's at home all the time.
Hattie (*appalled*) What?
Dora He's retired. He's sold the shop. So he'll be here all day.
Hattie All day? Father here all day?
Lucy All day. Every day.
Hattie Let's kill him.

There is a shocked silence

Agnes That was a very foolish and wicked thing to say. Now go along.
Hattie Well, in "Lady Carrington's Casket" . . .
Agnes Run along!

Hattie goes out

Dora What terrible things she says. Doesn't she say terrible things, Mamma?
Agnes She's only a child. Her imagination runs away with her.

A bell rings

Lucy (*rising*) Oh Lord, what have I forgotten now?
Agnes You go, Dora. I want to talk to Aunt Lucy.
Dora Must I?
Agnes Yes, quickly, or you'll put him in a bad mood. Think of Hattie and her verbs.
Dora Oh, Lord.

Dora goes out

Agnes (*slowly*) I suppose he'll come and tell me himself about having retired. What are his plans, did he say?

Lucy Oh, yes, he said. He's going to take a well-earned rest and give his home and family the benefit of his presence.

Agnes I see. He means well, of course. I'm sure he wants the best for us all.

Lucy Oh, I'm sure he does.

Agnes You see, he was very strictly brought up.

Lucy Yes.

Agnes He is severe, but severity is no bad thing in a man. He has such very high standards.

Lucy I don't think high standards are very easy to live with, Agnes. I think rather low standards must be—well—nicer really.

Agnes I'm afraid he will never change. High standards and a sense of duty—that's what he said we would have in our home. It sounded quite pleasant at the time.

Lucy Only it's him that's got the high standards and us that are supposed to have the sense of duty.

Agnes A man of decision. He likes to be thought a man of decision.

Lucy And he's decided to retire.

Agnes I've often thought I might turn out to be a woman of decision; if ever anything needed deciding, that is.

Lucy Edward decides everything here, anyway.

Agnes Isn't it funny how queer a word sounds when you keep on saying it. Decide. Decision. It seems to lose its meaning.

There is a tap at the door and Jessie comes in

Jessie Has Hattie gone in to Mr Bristow?

Agnes Yes.

Jessie (*anxiously*) I think she really has got *connaître* right now. I looked it up in the book to make sure. The trouble is she gets so nervous she forgets things.

Lucy It helps if you teach her right in the first place.

Jessie That was only once and the past imperfect is so difficult.

Lucy But you let Hattie take the blame.

Jessie (*distressed*) I know, I know it was wrong, but supposing he dismissed me? I've nowhere to go.

Agnes Lucy, please. And I seem to remember something about a broken moustache cup . . .
Lucy All right. I'm sorry, Jessie. I know I was just as bad. The trouble is he's so frightening, you just say the first thing you think of, to get out of it.

Hattie bursts in

Hattie Oh, Miss Plumb, oh what shall we do? The most awful thing . . .
Agnes What is it, what is it, dear? Have you forgotten your verbs?

Hattie rushes to her mother

Hattie No, it's far worse than that. He hasn't even heard them yet. We're going to do them in the morning, he says—because —because—he's going to dismiss Miss Plumb and attend to my education himself. I can't bear it. Oh, Mamma, I can't bear it.
Jessie Dismiss me! Oh!
Hattie And teach me himself! Oh, poor Miss Plumb! (*She flings her arms round Jessie*)
Lucy And poor Hattie.
Hattie (*to Jessie*) Let's run away, both of us. I've got three-and-ninepence in my money-box. We could live with the gypsies . . . I'd rather do anything than do lessons with father.
Agnes Hush, darling, hush. Of course you can't run away. We'll think of something. I promise you we'll think of something.
Hattie What is there to think of? All I can think of . . .

Dora comes in

Lucy (*looking up quickly*) What did he want?
Dora You'd given him the wrong teaspoon. You know he likes his special silver one.
Lucy I was in such a rush. Was he very cross?
Dora Not so very. He just said things would be different in future, and the house would be properly run at last, and there'd have to be an end to slipshod behaviour and slovenliness . . .
Lucy Slovenliness!
Dora There was a tea-stain on his tray cloth.
Lucy I know. I couldn't get it out. It was under the plate, though.

Dora Don't you know father yet? He looks under plates. What's the matter with Hattie?

Lucy Your father's going to teach her himself from now on.

Dora How awful! Oh, poor old Hattie. But what about Jessie?

Jessie He's going to dismiss me.

Dora Oh, no. Oh, Jessie, whatever will you do?

Jessie Try and get another post, I suppose, as soon as I can.

Dora If you go, I'll have no-one to talk to.

Hattie Let's all three run away. You can come with us if you like, Dora—with me and Miss Plumb.

Agnes Don't be silly, dear. Now run up to the schoolroom and Miss Plumb will come in a minute.

Hattie I'll wait for her. It's dark.

Jessie It's all right, Hattie, I left the schoolroom door open, you can see the light.

Hattie But it's still dark at the top of the stairs. I don't like it. I always think something's going to jump out at me.

Agnes It is dark there. I wish your father would let us leave the gas on. It's dangerous.

Lucy There'll be an accident one of these days.

Agnes Well, go up with Hattie, Jessie. We'll talk things over later on.

Dora I'll come too, I want to talk to Jessie.

Agnes Go up quietly.

Hattie and Jessie go out and Dora starts to follow them

Dora (*pausing at the door*) Oh, and father said don't forget his indigestion mixture.

Lucy As if I ever did.

Dora And be sure to shake the bottle.

Dora goes out

Lucy I always shake the bottle.

Agnes Better get it now. (*Giving Lucy a small key from the bunch*) Here you are.

Lucy unlocks the corner cupboard

(*Casually*) While you're there, get out my laudanum, will you dear?

Lucy (*concerned*) Why? Have you got the toothache?

Agnes No, not at the moment. I just want to see how much there is there.

Lucy It's nearly full. I only got it last week. ((*She opens the cupboard and takes out a large bottle of white medicine and a small dark green bottle*)

Agnes (*idly*) How does Edward take his medicine?

Lucy How?

Agnes I mean, does he sip it, or what?

Lucy Oh, he drinks it in one gulp. He doesn't like it, I know. And last week he made me take it back to the chemist, because it tasted different from usual, but Mr Spenlow said it was just the same, and that with Edward smoking so many cigars, it was a wonder he could taste anything.

Agnes I see. (*She takes the laudanum bottle and holds it to the light*) Well, put this into Edward's mixture, then, will you Lucy?

Lucy Agnes! It's poison!!

Agnes Well, not a very serious poison, is it? Look how much I've taken for my toothache.

Lucy A drop at a time.

Agnes So I know the good of it. It has a very calming effect. One wouldn't wish the excitement of retiring to be too much for him.

Lucy (*taking the bottle*) How much shall I put in?

Agnes All of it.

Lucy All! But the bottle's . . .

Agnes No, wait a moment. Not quite all. Leave a drop in the bottom, in case I get the toothache.

Lucy (*doubtfully*) Are you sure?

Agnes Yes, I'm quite sure. Oh, and Lucy, wash the glass extra well, won't you?

Lucy (*with the trace of a smile*) Oh, yes. Edward is very fussy about glasses.

Lucy goes out as the bell rings

Agnes leans back and the room darkens a little

Hattie comes in quietly

Hattie Mamma, you're not asleep, are you?

Agnes No, dear, just thinking. Don't keep running up and down stairs, dear. You know it annoys father.

Hattie I want to borrow a needle out of Dora's work-box.

Agnes Haven't you got one in your own work-box?

Hattie I can't find one, and Miss Plumb's work-box is in her bedroom, and it's dark up there. Let me find one of Dora's.

Agnes Very well then, but put it back. What are you sewing?

Hattie A shroud for Arabella.

Agnes A shroud! My dear child.

Hattie is turning things out of the work-box which Dora has left on the table

You really are dreadfully morbid. Does Arabella really need a shroud? She didn't seem very far gone to me, only her nose a bit melted. Let me look at her.

Hattie No. She is far gone. I'm going to bury her under the plane tree.

Agnes Well, I don't know, I'm sure. Don't rummage about like that, Hattie. Pass me the box.

Hattie gives the work-box to Agnes

It's untidy enough as it is. No wonder Dora gets in such a muddle with her sewing. (*She holds up a small needle*) Will this do?

Hattie No, it's far too tiny. I want a strong one. One of these. (*She takes a darning-needle*)

Agnes Those are darning-needles.

Hattie I'm only going to do big stitches. Shrouds don't get hard wear.

Agnes Poor Arabella, do bring her to me, darling. She was such an expensive doll.

Hattie No. She's had the last rites.

Agnes Dear me. I'm sure you shouldn't play these games, Hattie. Funerals and last rites.

Hattie They're not games. Miss Plumb's going to make her a proper coffin out of a shoebox and I shall read the funeral service and sing a hymn.

Agnes It sounds most irreverent. Still, if it's a comfort to you. I know you loved Arabella.

Hattie Mamma, which side is a person's heart on? Do you
   know?
Agnes Really, Hattie, what questions you ask. Well brought-up
   young ladies don't need to know things like that.
Hattie Yes, but which side?
Agnes The right side, dear, Yes, I'm sure it's the right side.
Hattie There now. Miss Plumb said it was the left side. I knew
   she was wrong.
Agnes I'm afraid she was, dear, but really it's not very important
   —is it? Not like French verbs.
Hattie That depends.

Dora comes in with a ball of string in her hand

Dora (*looking on the table*) Where's my work-box gone? (*She
   sees Agnes has it*) Oh, are my scissors there, Mamma?
Agnes What have you got there, Dora? String? You're surely
   not going to cut string with your embroidery scissors?
Dora (*impatiently*) It won't matter for once. Jessie's packing up a
   parcel to send to her sister.
Agnes But there's no hurry, is there? It won't go tonight.
Dora (*taking the box to the table*) She wants to get it done now,
   because there won't be time in the morning. (*She hunts in the
   work-box*) And father will be going up to change into his
   smoking-jacket soon. What happened about your French verbs,
   Hattie? You weren't in there a minute.
Hattie No, he's going to hear them in the mornings, from now on.
Dora I see. He wants to enjoy being beastly to you over his
   bacon and eggs, instead of his tea and toast. (*She turns out the
   work-box frantically*)
Agnes Dora—mind what you're doing. He can't have finished his
   tea yet. You've put his smoking-jacket out, have you?
Dora Yes, I just don't want to meet him in the hall, that's all.
Hattie I don't want to meet him anywhere.
Dora (*finding the scissors*) Here they are.

*There is the sound of a door opening and heavy footsteps going up
the hall*

   That's him going up now. He's early.

They listen anxiously as the footsteps pass the door

Hattie P'raps his toast wasn't right. He'll be in a terrible mood.

Dora goes to the door, opens it a crack, and listens as the footsteps disappear up the stairs

Dora There, he's gone into the bedroom.
Hattie Don't be long with that parcel. I want Jessie to make a coffin for Arabella. I say, she's not using that box is she?
Dora (*vaguely*) Box?
Hattie For the parcel. The one she's sending to her sister.
Dora Oh no. No. You'd better come upstairs with me, Hattie, it's quite dark now.
Hattie Yes, I'm going to sew my shroud by the schoolroom fire.
Dora (*startled into paying attention*) Your shroud? Are you going to kill yourself?
Hattie I mean Arabella's, silly. Though I might as well be dead, what with father and the past imperfect.
Agnes Hattie, please don't talk so much nonsense. And go up quietly, both of you. Oh, give me your work-box, Dora.

Dora takes the work-box to Agnes and then goes out with Hattie

Agnes tidies the work-box peacefully

Lucy comes in

Ah, Lucy. Turn the gas up a little, dear, would you? I can hardly see what I'm doing.

Lucy puts the two medicine bottles on the table

Lucy, the heart is on the right side of the body, isn't it? Hattie wanted to know.
Lucy Dear me no. The left side, dear. If you'd had palpitations as badly as I have, you'd know that.
Agnes There now. I was blaming Jessie for making mistakes, and now I've told her something wrong myself.
Lucy (*turning up the gas lamps with shaking hands*) I can't see that it matters.
Agnes That's better. Put the bottles away now, dear, and give me the key.

Lucy does so

You look flushed, Lucy. I wonder if you have a fever.

Lucy (*tremulously*) I—I don't think so, dear.

Agnes Why you're trembling! You'll have to go and see Dr Gallagher.

Lucy I don't think it would be much good going to see him, dear. He's practically stone deaf, and I don't think he can see very well.

Agnes Yes, he's getting old, poor Dr Gallagher. But he's very kind and understanding. That's important too. I feel he's so reliable, somehow.

Lucy If I needed a doctor, I think I would ask for his new partner, Dr Moss. He's very nice, and up-to-date as well, I should think.

Agnes (*alert*) I didn't know he'd got a partner. Why didn't you tell me?

Lucy I didn't think you wanted to know.

Agnes Lucy, if anything . . .

Suddenly there is a series of bumps and crashes, as if a heavy body is falling down the stairs

Lucy (*springing up*) He's fallen downstairs.

Agnes (*calmly*) It does sound like it.

Lucy I'd better go.

Agnes No, wait.

There is complete silence

Lucy (*after a pause*) I *must* see what's happened.

Agnes Certainly not, Lucy, you know how he hates to be disturbed.

Lucy I—I wonder if he came over dizzy at the top of the stairs?

Agnes I wonder.

Lucy Like in "Lady Rowena's Revenge".

Agnes I don't know what you mean, Lucy. Now sit down please.

Lucy But, Agnes, he may be seriously hurt.

Agnes On the other hand he may not. We can only hope.

There is the sound of hurrying feet then Dora rushes in

Dora Mamma, it's father. He's fallen downstairs. I think—I think—Oh, Mamma! (*She sits at the table and covers her face with her hands*)

Jessie comes in

Jessie (*quietly*) I—I think he's—er—passed away, Mrs Bristow.
Agnes I had better come.

*Agnes gets up unsteadily for the first time and walks to the door
and goes out, followed timidly by Lucy*

Jessie (*in an urgent whisper*) Why did you take the string away?
I said I would do that. It wasn't fair for you to do it all on your
own.
Dora I didn't. I went to undo it, and it wasn't there. I thought
you'd done it.
Jessie Didn't you put it there then? Across the top step?
Dora No. You were going to put it there, weren't you?
Jessie No—I was only going to take it away. After all, he was
your father. You were going to tie it, and I was going to take
it away afterwards. Oh Dora you got it all mixed up.
Dora But it doesn't matter, does it? He fell down anyway.
Jessie So he did.

They stare at each other, half inclined to giggle

Dora P'raps we put the Evil Eye on him!

Agnes comes in

Agnes (*unemotionally*) I'm afraid there's no doubt. Lucy has gone
for Dr Gallagher. Oh, Dora go after her will you and tell her
to make sure it's Dr Gallagher, not the new partner? One wants
one's old family doctor at such a time.

Dora goes out

*Agnes, her walk noticeably stronger, goes to the chaise-longue
and sits*

Jessie, dear, would you go and fetch the tray from the study
and wash up the things, just for once, especially the medicine
glass? I do so dislike dirty glasses standing about, it looks so
slovenly. Do it at once, will you dear?

Dora comes in and Jessie slips out

Dora Dr Gallagher's coming. He was just getting out of a cab.

*A man's voice can be heard from the hall saying, "Now what's been
happening here?"*

Agnes Good. Tell him I'm too upset to see him tonight, will you?

Lucy comes in

Lucy (*tremulously*) Dr— Dr—Gallagher—is here, Agnes. Shall I show him in here after . . .?
Agnes No, dear, I don't feel like seeing him tonight. I'm sure you will do just as well.
Lucy But, Agnes . . .

Jessie comes in holding a medicine glass of opaque white mixture

Jessie Mr Bristow didn't take his medicine, Mrs Bristow. What shall I do with it?

Agnes and Lucy exchange amazed looks

Agnes Tell Dr Gallagher I'd rather see him tomorrow, Lucy.

Lucy goes out

Give me that, Jessie. (*She takes the medicine from Jessie, briskly pours it into the plant pot and conceals the glass behind a photograph frame*)
Jessie Don't you want me to wash up the glass, Mrs Bristow?
Agnes Later will do after all. Where is Hattie?
Jessie In the schoolroom. I told her to stay there.
Agnes Well, we must break the sad news to her, I suppose. When you go up, Jessie, you might light the gas on the landing. Oh dear, this will be a shock for the poor child. All that playing at funerals, and now a real one.
Jessie Do you wish me to tell her, Mrs Bristow?
Agnes No. That is a mother's duty, I fear.

Lucy comes in

Lucy Dr Gallagher's gone, Agnes. He said as soon as his son comes in he'll get him to help carry Edward into the front room. And then Mrs O'Reilly can come and lay him out. And we're to get in touch with Price and Morton's he said. Oh, and he told me to give you this. (*She hands Agnes the death certificate*)
Agnes Cause of death—Heart failure. How strange, I never knew he had anything wrong with his heart.

Lucy He might have gone on for years, the doctor said. The only thing was—his heart was on the wrong side.
Agnes On the wrong side?
Lucy The right instead of the left. Always had been.
Agnes I didn't know you could have your heart on the wrong side.
Lucy It's quite rare, the doctor said. He seemed to think it was interesting.
Agnes It is. Very interesting.

Hattie comes in quietly and stands framed in the doorway. Dora, Agnes and Lucy stare at her

There is a moment's silence. Hattie goes over to the work-box and replaces the darning-needle

Hattie There you are, Dora. I promised I'd put it back when I'd finished with it.

There is a pause

Agnes Well, there doesn't seem much we can do for the moment.
Lucy We could have a cup of tea—unless . . .

The same idea strikes them all. Agnes hands the book to Jessie and they take the same places they had at the beginning of the play

Jessie (*reading*) "Lady Anne's eyelids fluttered, and with a gentle sigh she quietly breathed her last. Alas, dear Reader . . ."

CURTAIN

FURNITURE AND PROPERTY LIST

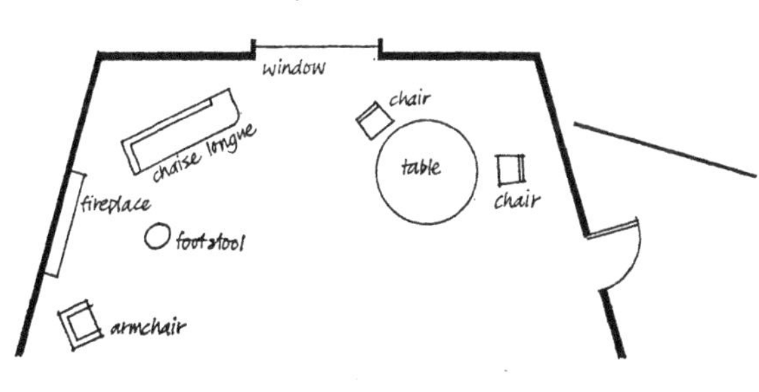

On stage: Chaise-longue. *On it:* cushion with 2 library books hidden
    behind it

    Table. *On it:* oil-lamp (practical), book of sermons, sewing
    work-box containing embroidery scissors, darning-needle,
    needles and other items to give a very cluttered impression

    2 chairs

    Footstool

    Armchair

    Aspidistra in pot

    Fireplace with draped mantelshelf. *On it:* photograph in
    frame

    Corner cupboard with a lock (practical). *In it:* large bottle of
    white opaque mixture and a small dark green poison
    bottle

    Garment in the process of being sewn badly **(Dora)**

    Book **(Jessie)**

    Doll **(Hattie)**

    Further dressing may be added at the director's discretion in
    order to convey the idea of a crowded Victorian parlour.

Off stage: Ball of string **(Dora)**

    Medicine glass containing opaque white mixture **(Jessie)**

    Death certificate **(Lucy)**

Personal: **Agnes:** bunch of keys in pocket

LIGHTING PLOT

Property fittings required: gas lamps either side of the mantelpiece, oil lamp on the table, bright glow from the fire stage right

Interior. A parlour. The same scene throughout

To open: Reasonably bright light from the oil and gas lamps

Cue 1	**Dora** turns the oil lamp down *Reduce lighting*	(Page 4)
Cue 2	**Agnes** leans back *The room darkens a little*	(Page 13)
Cue 3	**Lucy** turns up the gas lamps *Bring up the lighting*	(Page 16)

EFFECTS PLOT

MADE AND PRINTED IN GREAT BRITAIN BY
LATIMER TREND & COMPANY LTD PLYMOUTH

MADE IN ENGLAND